ATLANTA
FALCONS

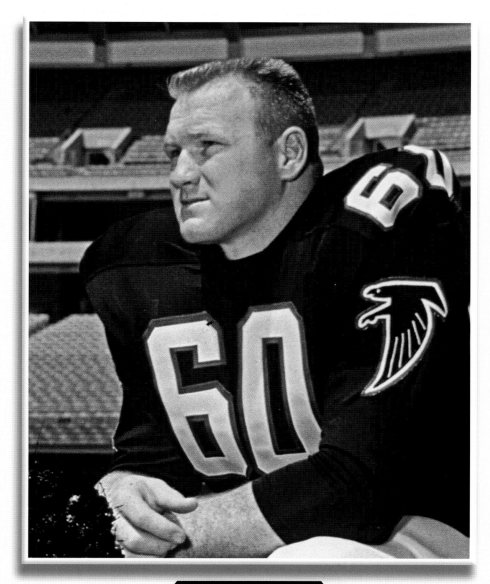

by Dave McMahon

Printed in the United States of America,
North Mankato, Minnesota
062010
092010

 THIS BOOK CONTAINS AT LEAST 10% RECYCLED MATERIALS.

Editor: Matt Tustison
Copy Editor: Nicholas Cafarelli
Interior Design and Production: Kazuko Collins
Cover Design: Kazuko Collins

Photo Credits: Evan Pinkus/AP Images, cover; NFL Photos/AP Images, 1, 15, 17, 18, 21, 25, 42 (top), 42 (middle), 42 (bottom), 44, ; Beth A. Keiser/AP Images, 4; David Stluka/AP Images, 7; Ed Reinke/AP Images, 8; John Bazemore/AP Images, 11, 37; AP Images, 12, 23; John Dickerson/AP Images, 26, 47; Spencer Weiner/AP Images, 28, 43 (top); Steven Senne/AP Images, 30; David Stluka/AP Images, 33; Alan Mothner/AP Images, 34; Darren Hauck/AP Images, 39, 43 (middle); John Amis/AP Images, 41, 43 (bottom)

Library of Congress Cataloging-in-Publication Data

McMahon, Dave.
  Atlanta Falcons / Dave McMahon.
    p. cm. — (Inside the NFL)
  Includes index.
  ISBN 978-1-61714-002-0
  1. Atlanta Falcons (Football team—History—Juvenile literature. I. Title.
  GV956.A85M37 2011
  796.332'6409758231—dc22

2010013673

TABLE OF CONTENTS

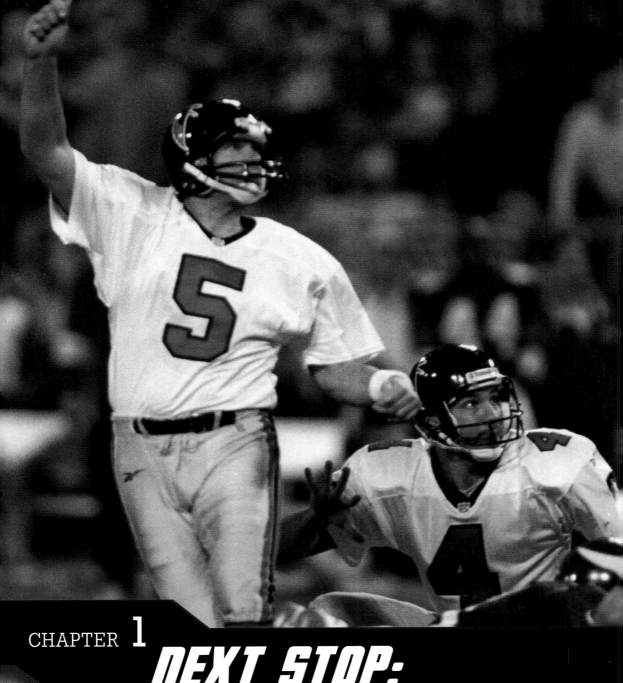

CHAPTER 1

NEXT STOP: SUPER BOWL

When Morten Andersen's 38-yard field goal sailed through the uprights on January 17, 1999, the Atlanta Falcons landed in unknown territory. They were thrilled. They were going to the Super Bowl for the first time in team history.

A 30–27 victory in overtime against the Minnesota Vikings in the National Football Conference (NFC) Championship Game not only secured a berth for the Falcons in Super Bowl XXXIII. It raised expectations for the team. Now fans knew how far the Falcons could go.

"We shocked the world! We shocked the world! Atlanta's on fire, we're going to Miami," Falcons linebacker Jessie Tuggle said. "No one thought we would be where we are right now, playing in the NFC championship. But not only did we come here to play in it, we came here to win it."

THE FALCONS' MORTEN ANDERSEN AND DAN STRYZINSKI WATCH ANDERSEN'S 38-YARD FIELD GOAL IN OVERTIME OF THE 1998 NFC TITLE GAME.

The 1998 season shaped up to be a gem for the Falcons. They ended the regular season with a team-best 14–2 record and nine wins in a row. Then came the NFC title game. The final score at the Hubert H. Humphrey Metrodome in Minneapolis could only begin to tell of the drama.

The 15–1 Vikings were playing at home and ready to pounce on the Falcons. During the regular season, Minnesota had scored 556 points, a National Football League (NFL) record.

"No one gave us a chance. Literally, not a chance," Falcons defensive end Travis Hall later said. "Back then, even though we went 14–2, no one gave us a chance. Everyone was saying the Vikings were the greatest team since the '72 Dolphins, maybe the greatest team ever."

Atlanta seemed to be next in the line of prey. No chance. Well, actually there had been a good chance that the Falcons would be flying south with a loss.

Gary Anderson tried to give the Vikings a 10-point lead with a 38-yard field goal of his own with less than three minutes to play in regulation. The kick, though, sailed wide by about a

ATLANTA'S MORTEN ANDERSEN CELEBRATES HIS GAME-WINNING FIELD GOAL AGAINST MINNESOTA IN THE 1998 NFC CHAMPIONSHIP GAME.

foot. Anderson had been perfect on field goals in the regular season and postseason. He had made all 39 of his field-goal attempts until what turned out to be his last kick of the season.

Making use of another chance to score, the Falcons drove 71 yards in eight plays to tie the game at 27–27. Atlanta quarterback Chris Chandler was playing on an injured ankle. Still, he connected with Terance Mathis on a 16-yard touchdown pass with 49 seconds to play in regulation.

Minnesota had taken a 27–17 lead less than two minutes into the fourth quarter. Andersen responded with a 24-yard field goal. Anderson's

FALCONS QUARTERBACK CHRIS CHANDLER PASSES IN THE NFC CHAMPIONSHIP GAME. CHANDLER THREW FOR 340 YARDS AND THREE TOUCHDOWNS.

WHAT NOISE?

Much had been made of the crowd noise that the Falcons could expect to hear at the Metrodome in the NFC Championship Game. But there is no better way to silence a crowd than to make a big play.

The Falcons were deep in their own territory with about two minutes left in regulation. They escaped the danger zone when quarterback Chris Chandler connected with tight end O.J. Santiago for 15 yards. Chandler then silenced the crowd again two plays later on a 26-yard pass to Santiago that brought the ball near midfield.

The crowd was very quiet after Chandler found Terance Mathis for a 16-yard touchdown pass to tie the score at 27–27 with 49 seconds left in regulation.

Finally, you could have heard a pin drop in the Metrodome after Morten Andersen's game-winning kick in overtime sent the Falcons to the Super Bowl.

miss for the Vikings kept the score at 27–20, setting the stage for Chandler. For the game, he finished with 340 yards and three touchdowns passing.

In overtime, the Vikings stalled on both of their possessions. A punt put the ball into Chandler's hands one last time. That was enough to bring the Falcons to their first Super Bowl.

"We deserve the same amount of respect that they [the Vikings] did," Atlanta cornerback Michael Booker said. "But when we got here, we found they were already selling tickets for the Super Bowl. We came here to spoil a lot of trips."

The trip to the Super Bowl was the high point in team history. Fans in the southeastern region of the United States showed that season that they could support a professional football team. In fact, for decades they had known that an NFL team in Atlanta would work. In the 1960s, they had tried for years to bring a team to Georgia. Finally, they celebrated their selection as an NFL franchise in 1965. It was the beginning of a long and bumpy road to the Super Bowl.

COACH DAN REEVES WAS BACK ON ATLANTA'S SIDELINE FOR THE NFC TITLE GAME. HE HAD UNDERGONE MAJOR HEART SURGERY THE MONTH BEFORE.

The National Football League
Certificate of Membership
NFL
This is to Certify That
The Atlanta Falcons Football Club

Owning and operating a Professional Football Club has by proper action of The National Football League, been duly nominated and admitted into membership in that League and has complied with Article III.

This Certificate

Endorses the right of The Five Smiths, Inc. to represent the City of Atlanta, Georgia in The National Football League in keeping with the Constitution and By-Laws. This membership may be terminated as provided by the Constitution.

CHAPTER 2
GETTING STARTED

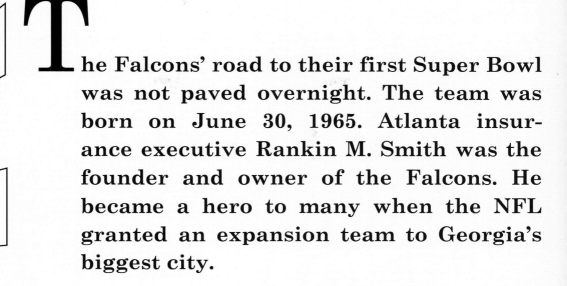

The Falcons' road to their first Super Bowl was not paved overnight. The team was born on June 30, 1965. Atlanta insurance executive Rankin M. Smith was the founder and owner of the Falcons. He became a hero to many when the NFL granted an expansion team to Georgia's biggest city.

Smith had been away from his insurance office on the day of the Falcons' birth. When he returned to work the next day, more good news awaited him. More than 1,000 people had called the office to buy tickets.

A contest to name the team was held over the next several weeks. A few fans had submitted the nickname "Falcons." Here is how schoolteacher Julia Elliott of Griffin, Georgia, described

TICKETS ANYONE?

The Falcons sold 45,000 season tickets their first season. Before that, the record for most season tickets sold for a first season was held by Minnesota, at 26,000 tickets in 1961.

NFL COMMISSIONER PETE ROZELLE, *LEFT*, PRESENTS A CERTIFICATE OF MEMBERSHIP TO FALCONS OWNER RANKIN M. SMITH ON FEBRUARY 15, 1966.

NOT SO FAST

The NFL was not the only league that had its sights set on Atlanta. The American Football League (AFL) also believed that football would be a success in the city.

In fact, two different groups reportedly applied for ownership of an AFL team in Atlanta. One group of Atlanta businessmen was awarded an AFL team on June 7, 1965.

NFL commissioner Pete Rozelle got word of the AFL's interest in Atlanta and quickly flew to the city. The NFL was very interested in placing a team in the South. Rozelle wanted to stop the rival league's claim on the city.

Rozelle forced the city—which owned the stadium that the team would play in—to make a choice. A little more than three weeks later, insurance executive Rankin M. Smith spread word that the team would become a member of the NFL. Smith paid $8.5 million for the team.

her choice of "Falcons": "The Falcon is proud and dignified, with great courage and fight. It never drops prey. It is deadly and has a great sporting tradition."

Football fans in Georgia were eager to fill Atlanta-Fulton County Stadium.

Smith's next step was to name the team's first head coach. He chose Norb Hecker, a former assistant coach with the Green Bay Packers. The Falcons' preseason debut took place on August 27, 1966, in Columbia, South Carolina. On that day, Atlanta beat the San Francisco 49ers 24–17.

By the time the regular season began, the Falcons were faced with more difficult

LINEBACKER TOMMY NOBIS, SHOWN IN 1968, WAS SELECTED TO THE PRO BOWL FIVE TIMES WITH ATLANTA.

challenges. They earned their first victory on November 20 in a 27–16 win over the New York Giants at Yankee Stadium.

Linebacker Tommy Nobis, a former University of Texas standout, was the Falcons' first draft pick. He provided the team with hope by being selected as the NFL Rookie of the Year.

Unfortunately for their fans, the Falcons were not on the winning end of many games during their first few years in the league. Their first season in 1966 ended with a 3–11 record.

It got even worse in 1967, when Hecker's team finished 1–12–1. Just three games into the 1968 season, former NFL star quarterback Norm Van Brocklin replaced Hecker as coach. The results were not much better in Van Brocklin's first season, as the Falcons went 2–12.

In 1971, Van Brocklin had plenty of reasons to believe things were looking up for the Falcons. In February, he had been elected to the Pro Football Hall of Fame for his play at quarterback with the Los Angeles Rams and Philadelphia Eagles. By December, he was guiding the Falcons to their first winning season in team history. Atlanta finished with a 7–6–1 record.

The Van Brocklin era featured two winning seasons. The Falcons went 9–5 in 1973. However, eight games into the 1974 season, Van Brocklin was fired as coach.

Back-to-back 4–10 seasons in 1975 and 1976 were highlighted mainly by running back Dave Hampton. He became the first Falcon to rush for 1,000 yards when he chalked up 61 in the 1975 season finale. He ended the season with 1,002 yards.

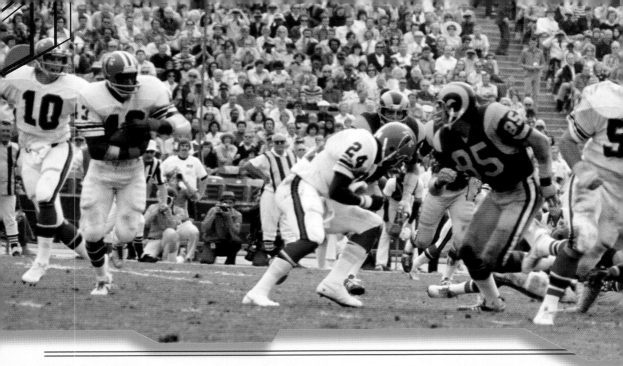

THE FALCONS' DAVE HAMPTON CARRIES THE BALL AGAINST THE RAMS IN 1975. HAMPTON RAN FOR MORE THAN 1,000 YARDS THAT SEASON.

Marion Campbell and Pat Peppler coached the team in the mid-1970s. The Falcons continued to struggle. However, with their fifth coach, they were primed to make the move from doormat to playoff contender.

Leeman Bennett, a former offensive assistant with the Rams, was hired as the Falcons' coach in 1977. He would complete six seasons with the team,

leading Atlanta to three playoff trips.

THE FUTURE'S ARRIVAL

The Falcons knew things were not going their way when they went into the 1975 NFL Draft. They made a trade with Baltimore to obtain the first pick in the draft. The trade proved to be worthy. In exchange for the opportunity to draft quarterback Steve Bartkowski out of the University of California, Berkeley, the Falcons gave the Colts offensive lineman George Kunz and a draft pick. Bartkowski threw for 23,470 yards and 154 touchdowns during his 11 years with Atlanta.

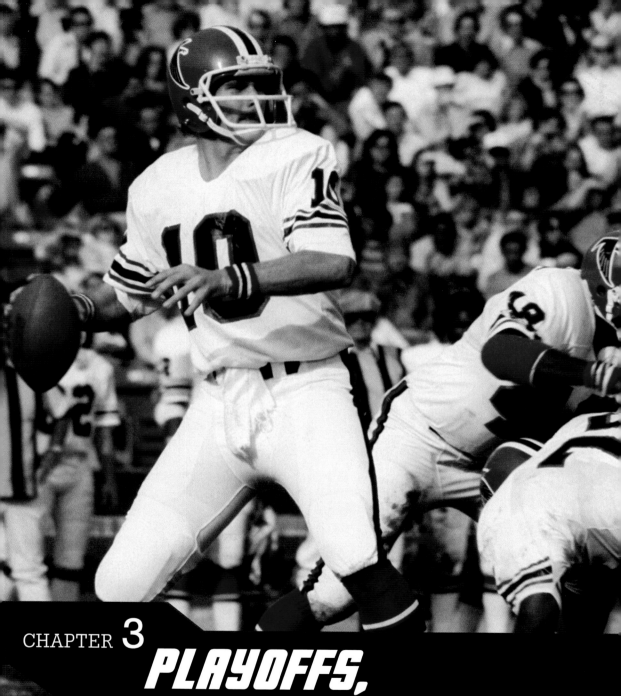

CHAPTER 3

PLAYOFFS, HERE WE COME

It did not take long to notice coach Leeman Bennett's impact on the Falcons. A defense that had struggled in previous years suddenly was being compared to some of the NFL's best defenses of all time. Quarterback Steve Bartkowski began to thrive under Bennett's guidance. The Falcons were headed in the right direction.

Claude Humphrey, a number one draft pick in 1968, continued to excel at defensive end. Rolland Lawrence gave the Falcons an interception threat at cornerback. In 1977, he started all 14 games in a Pro Bowl season and had seven interceptions. His impact on the Falcons' defense did not go unnoticed during his time manning the corner, from 1973 to 1980. He started every

GROWING PAINS

Steve Bartkowski's numbers were not so impressive at the beginning of his career in Atlanta. In 1976 and 1977, he combined to throw seven touchdown passes and 22 interceptions. When he led the Falcons to their first playoff appearance in 1980, Bartkowski threw 31 touchdown passes and 16 interceptions.

STEVE BARTKOWSKI LED THE FALCONS TO THEIR FIRST PLAYOFF SPOT, IN 1978. HE ALSO GUIDED THE 1980 AND 1982 TEAMS TO THE POSTSEASON.

game for seven seasons in a row and ended his career in Atlanta with 39 interceptions.

Defensive secondary coach Jerry Glanville helped Bennett mold a group that put up some of the stingiest numbers ever seen in the NFL. In the three previous seasons, the Falcons had allowed opponents to score a combined 312, 289, and 271 points. Those numbers changed quite a bit in 1977. In fact, the Falcons set a 14-game season record by allowing just 129 points that year. The result was seven wins, the most for the team since 1973.

Bennett had made his mark. Over the next five years, the Falcons advanced to the playoffs three times. The Falcons went 9–7 in 1978, boosted by their first shutout ever—a 14–0 win over Detroit—at Atlanta-Fulton County Stadium. Atlanta used other teams' misfortune to set up a prized bid in the playoffs that season. A mid-December loss by the Washington Redskins ensured the Falcons their first trip to the playoffs. Then, to top that off, the Los Angeles Rams beat Green Bay the next day. That meant the Falcons would play their first playoff game on their home field.

LEEMAN BENNETT, SHOWN IN 1982, TOOK OVER AS FALCONS COACH IN 1977. HIS ATLANTA TEAMS MADE THE PLAYOFFS THREE TIMES IN HIS SIX SEASONS.

Bartkowski made a name for himself in his first playoff game, a wild-card round contest against the Philadelphia Eagles. It was a rain-soaked game. Bartkowski threw for two touchdowns in the final eight minutes to give the Falcons a 14–13 victory. The Eagles missed a 34-yard field-goal try in the closing seconds. The win sent the Falcons on to the divisional round.

Against Dallas the next week, Atlanta led 20–13 at halftime. The Falcons' defense had knocked Cowboys quarterback Roger Staubach out of the game before halftime. Dallas, however, scored 14 unanswered points in the second half to post a 27–20 victory. The Falcons had the ball at the Cowboys' 32-yard line and faced a key fourth-and-one play in the fourth quarter. Dallas' defense held strong, and the Cowboys got the ball back.

A 6–10 season in 1979 hardly set the stage for what was to come in 1980. Second-year running back William Andrews set a team record with 1,308 rushing yards. Wide receiver Alfred Jenkins tallied 1,035 receiving yards, another record. And Bartkowski set the team season record with 3,544 passing yards and 31 touchdowns.

QUARTERBACK STEVE BARTKOWSKI LEAVES THE FIELD AFTER ATLANTA'S 30–27 PLAYOFF LOSS TO VISITING DALLAS ON JANUARY 4, 1981.

SUCCESS FOR SOME

The duo of William Andrews and Gerald Riggs in Atlanta's back-field gave Falcons fans plenty to talk about. The two players first started doing damage together during the 1982 season, which was shortened due to a players' strike. In the first game after the strike, Andrews gained 207 total yards. Riggs, a rookie, scored his first two touchdowns in a 34–17 win over the Rams.

The Falcons' 4–12 season in 1985 had some noteworthy individual performances. Billy "White Shoes" Johnson became the NFL's all-time leading punt returner. Riggs ran for 158 yards in the season finale. His 1,719 yards led the NFC and were the most in team history until 1998. Jamal Anderson rushed for 1,846 yards that year to break Riggs's record.

Riggs also had strong seasons in 1984 and 1986. He ran for 1,486 and 1,327 yards, respectively, those years.

The Falcons secured their first NFC West Division title with a 35–10 thumping of San Francisco. Bartkowski threw three touchdown passes. Andrews rushed for more than 100 yards for the sixth time that season. The Falcons' 12th victory of the season was also their ninth in a row. Both were club records.

In the divisional round of the playoffs against Dallas, Atlanta led 24–10 after three quarters. Still, the Falcons saw the Cowboys come back to win 30–27 in front of 60,022 people—Atlanta-Fulton County Stadium's largest crowd ever.

After a 7–9 season in 1981, Atlanta returned to the play-offs in 1982. That year, a strike by the NFL's players reduced the length of the regular season from 16 games to nine. Atlanta went 5–4 and advanced to the

THE FALCONS CHOSE RUNNING BACK GERALD RIGGS IN THE 1982 NFL DRAFT. IN 1985, HE RAN FOR 1,719 YARDS, A TEAM RECORD AT THE TIME.

playoffs for the third time. At the Metrodome against Minnesota, Atlanta had a 21–16 lead after three quarters in the wild-card game. The Vikings, however, came back to win 30–24.

Playoff opportunities, as the Falcons would learn in the coming years, are not chances to be taken lightly. It took Atlanta until 1991 to secure its first play-off victory on the road.

CHAPTER 4

DOME, SWEET DOME

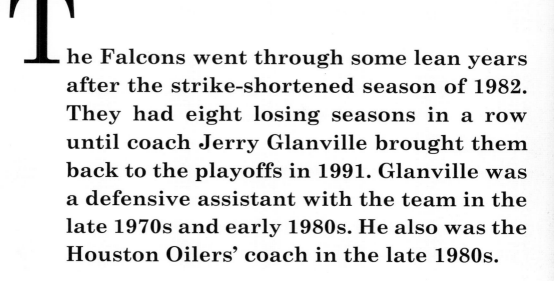

The Falcons went through some lean years after the strike-shortened season of 1982. They had eight losing seasons in a row until coach Jerry Glanville brought them back to the playoffs in 1991. Glanville was a defensive assistant with the team in the late 1970s and early 1980s. He also was the Houston Oilers' coach in the late 1980s.

The Falcons put together a five-game winning streak in 1991. They won eight of their final 11 games to gain a playoff spot with a 10–6 record. They won road games against all three of their division opponents.

The 1991 season also was the Falcons' last at Atlanta-Fulton County Stadium. A sellout crowd watched as Atlanta topped the Seattle Seahawks 26–13 in

PRIME TIME

In 1991, Falcons cornerback Deion "Prime Time" Sanders signed a baseball contract with the Atlanta Braves. He became the first pro athlete in 30 years to play two sports in the same city.

THE GEORGIA DOME OPENED IN 1992. IT REPLACED ATLANTA-FULTON COUNTY STADIUM AS THE FALCONS' HOME.

DEION SANDERS JOINED THE FALCONS IN 1989. HE QUICKLY BECAME A STANDOUT PUNT AND KICK RETURNER AND CORNERBACK.

the stadium finale to push the team's home winning streak to five games.

STOCK IS RISON

Andre Rison put up the quarter of a lifetime on November 17, 1991. The Falcons set a team record by scoring 33 points in a quarter. Rison scored 18 of those points on three touchdowns. He also tied a team record for most points scored by an individual in a game.

A 27–20 victory at New Orleans in a wild-card playoff game set up a showdown with Washington in the divisional round. Former Falcon Gerald Riggs scored two touchdowns to help the host Redskins to a 24–7 victory. Atlanta managed only 43 rushing yards. Quarterback Chris Miller threw four interceptions.

There was no time to worry about what might have been, however. The 1992 season would bring one of the most important dates in Falcons history.

On August 23, 1992, the Falcons played their first game in the Georgia Dome. The exhibition win over Philadelphia featured a bevy of stars. They included MC Hammer, who performed the team's "2 Legit 2 Quit" theme song. A halftime show included Georgia natives Travis Tritt, Alan Jackson, and Trisha Yearwood. John Denver sang the national anthem.

On September 6, Atlanta continued its Georgia Dome welcoming party. It scored on its first four possessions and beat the New York Jets 20–17.

The move into the Georgia Dome brought with it plenty of

PRIME TIME INDEED

Deion Sanders came to Atlanta with a flair for the dramatic. The Falcons took him fifth overall in the 1989 NFL Draft out of Florida State University.

At Florida State, Sanders excelled in football, baseball, and track. He was a two-time All-America cornerback and won the 1988 Jim Thorpe Award as the nation's top defensive back.

The multisport standout held out with the Falcons because of contract negotiations. Sanders then signed and attended just two practices before the season opener. In the first quarter, he returned a punt 68 yards for a touchdown. Earlier in the week, he had hit a home run for the New York Yankees. That made him the only athlete to hit a home run for a major league baseball team and score a touchdown in the NFL during the same week.

offensive firepower for the Falcons. They led the NFL in 1992 with a team-record 33 touchdown passes. Their 336 pass completions and 194 first downs also set team records.

Wide receiver Andre Rison had a record 93 receptions in 1992. He also became the first player in NFL history with 300 catches in his first four years in the league.

The second season inside the Georgia Dome, in 1993, led to a second straight 6–10 record. The points continued to pile up,

though. For the fourth season in a row, Atlanta scored more than 300 points. Rison set a team record among receivers with 15 touchdowns.

But a strong offense with a poor defense had led to bad results for the Falcons in previous years. Things were no different in 1993. Glanville resigned as coach after the season. He was replaced by former Falcons quarterback June Jones.

Jones had an unremarkable three-year tenure, going 7–9, 9–7, and 3–13. In 1995, however, the Falcons did pull off an impressive Georgia Dome moment to reach the playoffs.

Needing a win to qualify for the postseason, the Falcons edged defending Super Bowl champion San Francisco 28–27

ANDRE RISON BECAME THE FIRST NFL PLAYER WITH 300 RECEPTIONS IN HIS FIRST FOUR YEARS. HE SET AN ATLANTA MARK WITH 93 CATCHES IN 1992.

DEION KEEPS GOING

Deion Sanders continued to showcase his athletic spirit—and add to his frequent-flier miles—on October 11, 1992. On that day, he played two sports on the same day. The night before, a Saturday, he had played in the Braves' playoff game against the Pittsburgh Pirates. He then flew to Miami to play for the Falcons against the Dolphins on Sunday afternoon. He flew back to Pittsburgh for a Sunday night baseball game.

on Christmas Eve. Quarterback Bobby Hebert threw two touchdown passes to Terance Mathis. Mathis found his way into the end zone with 1:45 to play for the game winner. Hebert had replaced injured starter Jeff George.

The Falcons earned a playoff trip. However, they were handed a 37–20 loss at Green Bay. George was back for the game. But it was not enough.

George had a standout 1995 regular season, finishing with 4,143 passing yards. He became just the 18th quarterback in NFL history to throw for more than 4,000 yards in a season.

After a 3–13 record in 1996, Jones's time as coach came to an end. He was replaced by Dan Reeves, a man who would lead the Falcons to new heights.

JEFF GEORGE THROWS A PASS DURING ATLANTA'S 37–20 WILD-CARD PLAYOFF LOSS AT GREEN BAY ON DECEMBER 31, 1995.

CHAPTER 5

THE DIRTY BIRDS

When Dan Reeves took over as coach of the Falcons on January 20, 1997, his contract called for just five years of service. He stayed longer than he thought he would.

Reeves, a Georgia native, had coached the Denver Broncos to three Super Bowls.

A 7–9 record in 1997 to begin his time in Atlanta included a turnaround at the end of the season. The Falcons had started 1–7. However, they won six of their final eight games behind quarterback Chris Chandler's Pro Bowl season. The defense had 55 sacks, a team record.

The "Dirty Birds," as they became known, did not take long to launch into flight in the Super Bowl season of 1998. On November 8, the Falcons forced five turnovers and limited the New England Patriots to a record-low 18 rushing yards. All the buzz, however, was about their new end zone dance. Tight end O. J. Santiago and running back Jamal Anderson were the

FALCONS TIGHT END O. J. SANTIAGO DOES THE "DIRTY BIRD" DANCE AFTER A TOUCHDOWN IN 1998. ATLANTA WENT 14–2 THAT SEASON.

ringleaders of the move. They got plenty of practice with two touchdowns apiece.

"[The dance is] something that fans can identify with," Falcons receiver Terance Mathis said. "Fans may not know a player on this team, but they know what the 'Dirty Bird' is."

The mood among the Falcons was much more serious a month later, when Reeves underwent major heart surgery. Assistant coach Rich Brooks guided the

THE "DIRTY BIRD"

Fans who did not see the "Dirty Bird" dance on TV were given some instructions. First, "raise the roof" by bringing your right hand in the air. Then bring the arm down across your chest to form a wing. Perform the same motion with your left arm. Flap both arms together as if trying to fly. "From there, it's whatever you feel like," tight end O. J. Santiago said. "You can bounce with it, break it down, do whatever you want."

squad while Reeves was gone. Under Brooks, Atlanta claimed its second NFC West Division title in team history thanks to a 24–17 victory over Detroit.

The Birds were not ready to nest yet. After receiving a visit from a healing Reeves, the Falcons put an exclamation point on their season with a 38–16 victory over Dan Marino and the Miami Dolphins. Their club-record 14–2 season included an 8–0 record at home for the first time. The Falcons edged San Francisco 20–18 in their playoff opener, then beat Minnesota 30–27 in overtime in the classic NFC title game. Atlanta was on the way to its first Super Bowl.

By the time Super Bowl XXXIII had ended in Miami on January 31, 1999, though, John

ATLANTA'S JAMAL ANDERSON JUMPS INTO THE END ZONE FOR A TOUCHDOWN AGAINST INDIANAPOLIS IN 1998. ANDERSON HAD 16 TOUCHDOWNS THAT SEASON.

ANDERSON'S A GAMER

Jamal Anderson used his signature punishing moves to help the Falcons to a 24–17 victory over Detroit in 1998.

He was hit in the backfield on first-and-goal at the 1-yard line. Instead of taking a loss, he maintained his balance. He broke another tackle and then made his way into the end zone for the go-ahead touchdown with 6:57 left in the fourth quarter.

Anderson rushed for 5,336 yards and 34 touchdowns in an eight-year career with Atlanta. He ran for 1,846 yards in the Super Bowl season in 1998. Through 2009, that was the ninth-highest rushing total ever in the NFL.

Anderson, who played at the University of Utah, was not selected until the seventh round of the 1994 NFL Draft. He rushed for 1,000 yards in four different seasons for the Falcons. He suffered a career-ending knee injury in 2001.

Elway and the Denver Broncos were celebrating their second world title in a row. Atlanta lost 34–19 after being unable to rein in Elway, the Super Bowl Most Valuable Player.

The Falcons then went back to their old ways. They followed their Super Bowl season with records of 5–11 and 4–12.

Help, however, was on the way. Atlanta made a deal with the San Diego Chargers to secure the rights to the number one pick in the 2001 NFL Draft. The Falcons selected Michael Vick. He was a quarterback out of Virginia Tech who could pass and run well. He would play six seasons with Atlanta.

In February 2002, Arthur Blank bought the Falcons from longtime owner Rankin M. Smith. Blank was a cofounder of the Home Depot store chain.

ATLANTA QUARTERBACK MICHAEL VICK BREAKS AWAY FROM GREEN BAY DEFENDERS IN THE FALCONS' 27–7 PLAYOFF WIN ON JANUARY 4, 2003.

The Falcons went 9–6–1 in 2002 and earned a wild-card playoff berth. Atlanta defeated Green Bay 27–7 to become the first team ever to beat the Packers at home in a playoff game. The Falcons lost 20–6 at Philadelphia in the next round.

Reeves stepped down as coach toward the end of the 2003 season. Former San Francisco defensive coordinator Jim Mora became Atlanta's coach in 2004. The Falcons went 11–5 and won the NFC South Division title in Mora's first season. Atlanta routed visiting St. Louis 47–17

MICHAEL VICK

Michael Vick's best season came in 2004. Vick's 902 rushing yards were the third-highest total by a quarterback in NFL history. In the playoffs, he guided the Falcons to their second NFC Championship Game. Vick ran for 119 yards in a divisional playoff win over St. Louis. Against Philadelphia in the NFC Championship Game, Vick managed only 26 rushing yards in Atlanta's loss.

in the playoffs' divisional round before losing to host Philadelphia 27–10 in the NFC title game.

In April 2007, Vick was accused of being involved in an illegal dogfighting operation. It had been running in several states for more than five years. In August 2007, Vick pleaded guilty to federal felony charges. He admitted in court documents that he was involved in the dogfighting operation. He served 21 months in prison, followed by two months in home confinement.

Before he served his prison sentence, the three-time Pro Bowl selection passed for 11,505 yards and ran for another 3,859 in the equivalent of about five full seasons for the Falcons. After serving an NFL suspension, Vick signed with Philadelphia in 2009. He played in 12 games for the Eagles that season.

Quarterback Matt Ryan, meanwhile, appeared to be on the verge of making the Falcons a contender once again.

Ryan was the third overall pick in the 2008 NFL Draft. He and new coach Mike Smith led the Falcons to the playoffs in 2008 and a 9–7 record in 2009. They became the foundation for what Falcons fans hope will be a bright future in Atlanta.

MATT RYAN, TAKEN THIRD OVERALL BY ATLANTA IN THE 2008 DRAFT, THREW 38 TOUCHDOWN PASSES COMBINED IN HIS FIRST TWO NFL SEASONS.

1965	Owner Rankin M. Smith is awarded an NFL franchise for Atlanta for a cost of $8.5 million.
1966	The Falcons go 3–11 in their inaugural season.
1971	Atlanta wins its first nationally televised game with a 28–21 victory over Green Bay on *Monday Night Football*.
1971	The Falcons secure their first winning record with a 24–20 victory over New Orleans.
1973	The Falcons smash 35 team records in a 62–7 trouncing of New Orleans in the opener. They will go on to finish the season with a franchise-best 9–5 record.
1975	The Falcons select quarterback Steve Bartkowski as the number one draft choice.
1978	Atlanta clinches its first playoff berth with a 9–7 record and goes on to top Philadelphia in a wild-card game before losing to Dallas in the divisional round.
1980	The Falcons use a nine-game winning streak to post a 12–4 record on their way to their first NFC West Division title.
1984	Gerald Riggs takes over for Falcons all-time leading rusher William Andrews. Riggs sets a team record with 35 carries for 202 yards in a season-opening win against New Orleans.
1986	Atlanta starts the season with four wins in a row for the first time in team history.

1991	Cornerbacks Deion Sanders and Tim McKyer share the NFC lead in interceptions with six apiece. The Falcons play their final season at Atlanta-Fulton County Stadium.
1998	Coach Dan Reeves undergoes major heart surgery on the way to leading Atlanta to a 14–2 season and a division title. The team reaches its first Super Bowl in January 1999 but falls 34–19 to Denver.
2001	In his rookie season, quarterback Michael Vick throws for 785 yards and rushes for 289 yards in just eight games.
2002	The Falcons play their first season with Arthur Blank as owner. With a 27–7 victory, they become the first team to defeat Green Bay at Lambeau Field in the playoffs. Atlanta then loses 20–6 at Philadelphia in the divisional round.
2004	Under first-year coach Jim Mora, the Falcons win a division title for just the third time in team history.
2007	The NFL suspends Vick without pay after he pleads guilty to being involved in an illegal dogfighting operation. He will serve 21 months in prison.
2008	It is a new beginning as first-year coach Mike Smith and rookie quarterback Matt Ryan (drafted third overall) bring the Falcons back to the playoffs, only to lose to eventual NFC champion Arizona.
2009	For the first time in franchise history, the Falcons post consecutive winning seasons after winning their last game of the regular season to go 9–7.

QUICK STATS

FRANCHISE HISTORY

1966–

SUPER BOWLS

1998 (XXXIII)

NFC CHAMPIONSHIP GAMES
(since 1970 AFL-NFL merger)

1998, 2004

DIVISION CHAMPIONSHIPS
(since 1970 AFL-NFL merger)

1980, 1998, 2004

KEY PLAYERS
(position, seasons with team)

William Andrews (FB, 1979–83, 1986)
Steve Bartkowski (QB, 1975–85)
Bill Fralic (G, 1985–92)
Claude Humphrey (DE, 1968–74, 1976–78)
Mike Kenn (T, 1978–94)
Terance Mathis (WR, 1994–2001)
Tommy Nobis (LB, 1966–76)
Gerald Riggs (RB, 1982–88)
Andre Rison (WR, 1990–94)
Deion Sanders (CB/KR/PR, 1989–93)
Jessie Tuggle (LB, 1987–2000)
Jeff Van Note (C, 1969–86)
Michael Vick (QB, 2001–06)

KEY COACHES

Leeman Bennett (1977–82):
    46–41–0; 1–3 (playoffs)
Dan Reeves (1997–2003):
    49–59–1; 3–2 (playoffs)

HOME FIELDS

Atlanta-Fulton County Stadium
    (1966–91)
Georgia Dome (1992–)

* All statistics through 2009 season

"I'm gonna ask for so much money, the Falcons are gonna have to put me on layaway."
—Deion Sanders, after being selected fifth overall in the 1989 NFL Draft. Previously, Sanders had arrived at his final college game at Florida State University in a limousine, wearing a top hat and coattails.

Falcons quarterback Jeff George got into a heated argument with coach June Jones on the sideline during a game against the Philadelphia Eagles in September 1996. Television cameras caught the tantrum. Jones suspended George for the rest of the season. Atlanta released him a month later.

Atlanta's defense in 1977 took on a flavor rich in the southern tradition. Coach Leeman Bennett's defense was given the nickname of "Grits Blitz" on its way to allowing fewer than 10 points per game. The "Grits Blitz" allowed defensive players to rush the quarterback from nearly any position. The Falcons allowed just 129 points in 14 games that season. Grits are a southern breakfast staple, similar to porridge and made of ground corn.

"I am best described as a 'people coach.' I believe in knowing our people and going from there. People play the game, not Xs and Os."
—Leeman Bennett, who, after taking over as coach in 1977, led the Falcons to their first NFC West Division title in 1978

GLOSSARY

American Football League

A professional football league that operated from 1960 to 1969, when it became part of the National Football League.

berth

A place, spot, or position, such as in the NFL playoffs.

contender

A team that is considered good enough to win a championship.

contract

A binding agreement about, for example, years of commitment by a football player in exchange for a given salary.

doormat

A team that spends a long time at the bottom of the league standings.

draft

A system used by professional sports leagues to select new players in order to spread incoming talent among all teams.

firepower

The ability to score points in a variety of ways, including offensively, defensively, and on special teams.

franchise

An entire sports organization, including the players, coaches, and staff.

Pro Bowl

A game after the regular season in which the top players from the AFC play against the top players from the NFC.

ringleaders

Those people who start a trend or make decisions for a larger group of people.

rookie

A first-year professional athlete.

secondary

The defensive players who line up behind the linebackers to defend the pass and assist with run coverage.

FOR MORE INFORMATION

Further Reading

MacCambridge, Michael. *America's Game: The Epic Story of How Pro Football Captured a Nation.* New York, NY: Random House, 2004.

Rhoden, William C. *Third and a Mile: The Trials and Triumphs of the Black Quarterback.* New York, NY: ESPN Books, 2007.

Winkeljohn, Matt. *Tales from the Atlanta Falcons Sideline.* Champaign, IL: Sports Publishing LLC, 2005.

Web Links

To learn more about the Atlanta Falcons, visit ABDO Publishing Company online at **www.abdopublishing.com**. Web sites about the Falcons are featured on our Book Links page. These links are routinely monitored and updated to provide the most current information available.

Places to Visit

Falcons Training Complex
4400 Falcon Parkway
Flowery Branch, GA 30542
770-965-3115
www.atlantafalcons.com/Venues/Flowery_Branch.aspx
The Falcons have a self-contained training camp complex. Fans can attend preseason practice sessions.

Georgia Dome
1 Georgia Dome Drive Northwest
Atlanta, GA 30313
404-223-9200
www.gadome.com
The Falcons' home, the Georgia Dome seats 71,228. The team plays eight regular-season games here every year.

Pro Football Hall of Fame
2121 George Halas Drive Northwest
Canton, OH 44708
330-456-8207
www.profootballhof.com
This hall of fame and museum highlights the greatest players and moments in the history of the National Football League. Two players affiliated with the Falcons—running back Eric Dickerson and wide receiver Tommy McDonald—were enshrined as of 2010. Each was with the team for just one season.

INDEX

About the Author

Dave McMahon grew up in Newnan, Georgia, and attended Falcons games at Atlanta-Fulton County Stadium. A University of Notre Dame graduate, McMahon has written for newspapers, magazines, and sports Web sites. He lives in Eagan, Minnesota, with his wife and three children.